To: ....

From: ....

Cover and interior images: Fancy Photography / Veer

Published by Barbour Publishing, Inc., P.O. Box 719, Uhrichsville, Ohio 44683, www.barbourbooks.com

Our mission is to publish and distribute inspirational products offering exceptional value and biblical encouragement to the masses.

 Member of the
Evangelical Christian
Publishers Association

Printed in China.

M.O.L.
Meow Out Loud

BARBOUR
PUBLISHING

They MOL and we LOL!

A cat's life certainly has its funny moments.
From kitten cuteness to feline fabulousness,
our pets amuse us, keep us on our toes, and fill
our hearts with love. Here's a collection of kitty
quips, quotes, and inspiration guaranteed to put
a smile on the face of every feline's friend.

Humans: No fur, no paws, no tail. They run away from mice. They never get enough sleep. How can you help but love such an absurd animal?

An Anonymous Cat on Human Beings

My cat the clown: paying no mind to whom he should impress. Merely living his life, doing what pleases him, and making me smile.

Unknown

Who among us hasn't envied a cat's ability to ignore the cares of daily life and to relax completely?

Karen Brademeyer

If a dog jumps up into your lap,
it is because he is fond of you;
but if a cat does the same thing,
it is because your lap is warmer.

Alfred North Whitehead

Lord, thank You for the companionship of my cat. Teach me to be a better friend to the people around me every day. Amen.

Two people are better off than one, for they can help each other succeed. If one person falls, the other can reach out and help. But someone who falls alone is in real trouble. Likewise, two people lying close together can keep each other warm. But how can one be warm alone?

Ecclesiastes 4:9–11 NLT

As every cat owner knows, nobody owns a cat.
Ellen Perry Berkeley

There's no other sound like a purr, right by your ear as you are waking up. The slow lull of contentment. The paw half over the face. The seemingly effortless drone that announces to anyone close enough to hear, "Life is good."

Of all God's creatures, there is only one that cannot be made slave of the leash. That one is the cat. If man could be crossed with the cat it would improve the man, but it would deteriorate the cat.

Mark Twain

It is impossible to keep a straight face in the presence of one or more kittens.

Cynthia E. Varnado

Cats seem to go on the principle that it never does any harm to ask for what you want.

Joseph Wood Krutch

Simple cat pleasures:
a ball of yarn to chase, a feather to
capture, a flashlight's beam to pounce.

When cat and mouse agree,
the farmer has no chance.

English Proverb

If cats had wings,
there would be no
ducks in the lake.

Indian Proverb

Cat: The only domestic animal
man has never conquered.
Unknown

Good cat owners always introduce
their cats as members of the family.
Fluffy

Before a cat will condescend

To treat you as a trusted friend,

Some little token of esteem

Is needed, like a dish of cream.

T. S. Eliot

I can learn a lot from my cat, Father. His peaceful slumber reminds me that You invite me to find rest in You—no matter what else is going on in my life.

In peace I will lie down and sleep,

for you alone, LORD, make me dwell in safety.

Psalm 4:8

My Cat Has Got No Name

My cat has got no name
We simply call him Cat;
He doesn't seem to blame
Anyone for that.

For he is not like us
Who often, I'm afraid,
Kick up quite a fuss
If our names are mislaid.

Vernon Scannell

A kitten is so flexible that she is almost double; the hind parts are equivalent to another kitten with which the forepart plays. She does not discover that her tail belongs to her until you tread on it.

Henry David Thoreau

A shredded sofa is a small price to pay for having me to love.

Fluffy

When I was a small girl, I had a cat named April. April had a litter box, litter, food dishes, food, and water. Now I realize how deprived she was! Today's felines have condos, trees, towers, hammocks, cradles, playhouses, and tunnels. Some even have cat-sized sofas, chairs, and beds. Yet April loved me well, even in her poverty.

Unknown

Life is a constant battle between diet and dessert. I'm not overweight; I'm undertall.

Garfield

One good thing about lethargy. You don't have to work at it.

Garfield

Like annoying women who marry a man and then instantly want to reform him, cats have very firm ideas about what they want in a lifetime companion. . . . After all, they didn't choose you, they got stuck with you. Like mail-order brides, if they had hissed and spat and refused to be carried over the threshold, who knows what would have become of them?

Ingrid Newkirk

Cats only pretend to be domesticated if they think there's a bowl of milk in it for them.

Robin Williams

Father God, thank You for this little cat that—in some small way—shares Your loving comfort with me. Her soft presence soothes me, her purr calms my fears, and her snuggle brightens my day.

All praise to God, the Father of our Lord Jesus Christ. God is our merciful Father and the source of all comfort. He comforts us in all our troubles so that we can comfort others. When they are troubled, we will be able to give them the same comfort God has given us.

2 Corinthians 1:3–4 NLT

Oh loving puss, come hither and purr
Let me stroke your soft, warm fur.
Let me gaze into your loving eyes
How great their depth. . .how very wise.

What comfort your dear presence brings
I forget all sad, unhappy things.
Let no man live without this peace
Proof that God's wonders never cease.

Dutch Carrie

Why did God make dogs? So people would have someone look up to them. Why did God make cats? To keep us humble.

If cats could talk, they wouldn't.
Nan Porter

There is nothing in the animal world, to my mind, more delightful than grown cats at play. They are so swift and light and graceful, so subtle and designing, and yet so richly comic.

Monica Edwards

Cats are rather delicate creatures, and they are subject to a good many ailments, but I never heard of one who suffered from insomnia.

Joseph Wood Krutch

No matter how much the cats fight, there always seem to be plenty of kittens.

Abraham Lincoln

Cat Commandments:

Thou shalt never swallow a pill.

Thou shalt not eat cheap cat food.

Thou shalt occupy the most comfortable
spot in the room.

According to a recent poll of the worldwide cat population, the average feline does indeed feel superior to its human "owners." In fact, 53 percent of cats, spanning a range of species, expressed a strong belief that they would one day control the world.

Unknown

You may not be able to take a cat for a walk, but neither can you get a dog to purr.

Sometimes you're the cat.
Sometimes you're the litter box.

Lord, just as You are my Provider and Keeper, You have sent me this little, furry creature to provide food, shelter, and love. May I never take Your provision for granted.

The LORD is my shepherd, I lack nothing. He makes me lie down in green pastures, he leads me beside quiet waters, he refreshes my soul.

Psalm 23:1–3

Your cat will never threaten your popularity by barking at three in the morning. He won't attack the mailman or eat the drapes, although he may climb the drapes to see how the room looks from the ceiling.

Helen Powers

It's really the cat's house—
we just pay the mortgage.
Unknown

To err is human;
to get revenge, feline.

I have noticed that what cats most appreciate in a human being is not the ability to produce food, which they take for granted— but his or her entertainment value.

Geoffrey Household

The reason cats climb is so they can look down on almost every other animals— it's also the reason they hate birds.

K. C. Buffington

Kittens are God's opinion that we should laugh more.

People that hate cats will come back as mice in their next life.

Faith Resnick

Cats seem to know when a houseguest doesn't like cats. They choose his lap to jump in.

My Cat

My cat rubs my leg
And starts to purr
With a soft little rumble,
A soft little whir,
As if she had motors
Inside of her.

I say, "Nice Kitty,"
And stroke her fur,
And though she can't talk
And I can't purr,
She understands me,
And I do her.

Aileen Fisher

Cats find humans [to be] useful domestic animals.

George Mikes

Any household with at least one feline member has no need for an alarm clock.

Louise A. Belcher

God, thank You for showing me evidence of Your love in everyday life. You created pets to be our companions and friends—and through them I get a glimpse of Your love for me. Amazing!

May your unfailing love be my comfort, according to your promise to your servant. Let your compassion come to me that I may live, for your law is my delight.

Psalm 119:76–77

The litter box is great for my passive-aggressiveness. As soon as my owner cleans it, I get the urge to use it.

Snowball

A cat pours his body on the floor like water.

William Lyon Phelps

My husband said it was him or the cat. . . .
I miss him sometimes.

Unknown

Dogs come when they're
called. Cats take a message
and get back to you.

Mary Bly

I gave my cat a bath once. I thought she'd feel so much better. But in the end, we were both the worse for it, and I've never done it to either of us since. Though I have to admit that every so often we find ourselves in the bathroom at the same time, and I feel sure we both remember the horror.

Unknown

There was an old bulldog
named Caesar,
Who went for a cat
just to tease her;
But she spat and she spit,
Till the old bulldog quit.
Now when poor Caesar sees her,
he flees her.

Unknown

Who would believe such pleasure
from a wee ball o' fur?
Irish Saying

If stretching were wealth,
the cat would be rich.
African Proverb

"Pussycat, pussycat,
where have you been?"
"I've been to London
to look at the Queen."
"Pussycat, pussycat,
what did you there?"
"I frightened a little mouse
under the chair."

Mother Goose

I have learned a lot from my cat. When life is loud and scary, go under the bed and nap. When you want someone to notice you, sit on the book that person is reading. And if someone sits in your chair, glare at her until she moves.

Unknown

Father, when I see my cat sleeping peacefully in a sunbeam, I yearn for that rest. Help me to remember that You are my true source of peace today and every day.

*Search for peace,
and work to maintain it.*
Psalm 34:14 NLT

A computer and a cat are somewhat alike—they both purr and like to be stroked and spend a lot of the day motionless. They also have secrets they don't necessarily share.

John Updike

A cat is a lion in a jungle of small bushes.

Indian Proverb

Cat advice:
You can nap through most
of life's problems.

A kitten is chiefly remarkable
for rushing about like mad at
nothing whatsoever and generally
stopping before it gets there.

Agnes Repplier

Cats sleep anywhere, any table, any chair.

Top of piano, window ledge, in the middle, on the edge.

Open drawer, empty shoe, anybody's lap will do.

Fitted in a cardboard box, in the cupboard with your frocks.

Anywhere! They don't care! Cats sleep anywhere.

Eleanor Farjeon

Within minutes of his arrival, the new kitten has endeared himself to everyone. By the time he is one year old, he rejects all but the most expensive cat food and commandeers the best chair in the living room. On his tenth birthday, he has the master bed almost entirely to himself.

Vicky Halls

Cats make exquisite photographs. . . . They don't keep bouncing at you to be kissed, just as you get the lens adjusted.

Gladys Taber

My cat has a theory about the scratching post. In a nutshell it is, "Do not use it." When she passes the post, she looks at it with disdain and sticks her tail in the air. Then with an air of entitlement, she scratches the doorframe. Satisfied, she wanders off to take yet another nap.

Unknown

Even on the days my cat has an attitude,
I still know deep down she loves me, Father.
Please forgive me on the days when I have
an attitude toward You. I am thankful that
You know my heart.

*Love is patient and kind. . . . It does not
demand its own way. It is not irritable,
and it keeps no record of being wronged.
Love never gives up, never loses faith,
is always hopeful, and endures through
every circumstance.*

1 Corinthians 13:4–5, 7 NLT

The cat understands why some people prefer dogs: makes them both feel smart.
Pat Welch

A cat can be trusted to purr when she is pleased, which is more than can be said for human beings.
William Ralph Inge

Cats always know whether people like or dislike them. They don't always care enough to do anything about it.

Winifred Carrière

When my cats aren't happy, I'm not happy...because I know they're just sitting there thinking up ways to get even.

Percy Bysshe Shelley

The trick is to pretend to fall asleep
on their lap so they'll feel bad about
standing up and disturbing your slumber.

Advice from Fluffy

My owner calls me "Princess."
I call her "Food Opener."

Princess

When I play with my cat, who knows whether she is not amusing herself with me more than I with her.

Michel de Montaigne

Even overweight cats instinctively know the cardinal rule: when fat, arrange yourself in slim poses.

John Weitz

He's nothing much but fur
And two round eyes of blue,
He has a giant purr
And a midget mew.

Eleanor Farjeon

It's not the number of cats. . .
it's the number of litter boxes
you're prepared to live with.

Michael and Margaret Korda

Cat hair on my best coat,
Even on the mouse!
You live and eat and breathe cat hair,
When cats live in your house.

Unknown

God, help me to remember that just as You care for every living creature—human and animal—You ask me to do the same. Show me people and animals that need a pick-me-up, a little extra love, a little extra care—and make me humble enough to fulfill their needs.

"I am giving you a sign of my covenant with you and with all living creatures.... When I see the rainbow in the clouds, I will remember the eternal covenant between God and every living creature on earth."

Genesis 9:12, 16 NLT